Conversion Immersion

We Choose to be Chosen

Written by Donald Cassidy

(Daniel ben Avraham vSara)

Edited by Judith Cassidy

(Yehudit bat Avraham vSara)

Dedication

We dedicate this story to all humans who pray and who work for world peace. No kidding. We do this every day. We also dedicate this book to Rabbi Aaron Krauss and Cantor Ralph Goren, who continue to work and pray for a better world.

Editor's Note

This was not an easy book for my husband to write or for me to edit. I grew up attending Catholic grade school, high school, and college. I converted more than 60 years later because we were welcomed with open arms at Beth El. Judaism is often called "the first monotheistic religion," and other religions evolved from it, including Christianity renaming The Tanach (The Hebrew Bible) as "The Old Testament." Over the centuries, Roman Catholicism also borrowed many secular practices of holiday celebration from Judaism. For example, Easter eggs and candy occur in the spring following the Jewish holiday of Purim, which has celebrated with gifts and treats for thousands of years. The giving of gifts at Hanukkah is not practiced by all Jews, but certainly pre-dates the Christmas tradition of gift-giving.

The Christmas tree tradition started with a winter solstice celebration, a tradition of pagan and Germanic people. The tree was adopted by the Catholic Church, not to represent the birth of Jesus, but to incorporate the traditions of people who might then turn toward Catholicism. The evergreen tree remained a tradition in England. Even Queen Victoria had a tree in her castle. Evergreen trees are beautiful and are a tradition in our extended family households. I look forward to decorating my home during Hanukkah in addition to setting out a menorah both in our house and the outdoor menorah. An evergreen tree celebrates the holiday season and my family. This does not make me any less a Jew.

Author's Note

This narrative tells our conversion story, a married couple who were born and raised as members of Christian church congregations for more than 60 years. After one year of attending synagogue, studying Torah and Tanach, we both converted to Judaism on the same day in the year 2020 (5780). We tell many funny stories and several serious ones.

We respect all people for the choices we make to honor God, no matter what name we use: Adonai, Allah, God the Father, Hashem, Jesus Christ, The Great Spirit, Buddha, or any other name in any language to refer to God, the universal and connecting spirit of humanity. We also respect people who are agnostic or atheist.

Some of our stories might offend some readers. This is NOT our goal. We intend only to communicate that the world needs now more than ever to love our neighbors . . . a desire which has expression in all religions and cultures as far as we know. We must "study war no more" lest human beings go the way of many other extinct species on planet Earth.

To do this, we have left behind the Christian focus on the "promise" of attaining eternal life in Heaven. Instead, in our new Faith, we join all humans in trying to create a heaven here on Earth by showing our love of God through good deeds, the Golden Rule (found in both the Christian and Hebrew Bibles), and achieving this through kindness, generosity, and peace.

Table of Contents

SECTION ONE

THE BACK STORY

These chapters show what led us, a married Christian couple, to convert to Judaism on the same day

Chapter 1
We Met in Jail

From time to time, people ask how we met. Don answered, "We met in jail."

Judy frowned, then smiled. She explained that she had been working at the jail in Atlantic County, NJ, starting in 2007 as an R.N., and Don arrived there in 2011 as the new psychologist and Mental Health Director.

Within a few days, one of the medical staff members said, "Hey, Miss Judy. See that new doctor over there? Isn't he handsome? Well, he's single. You've gotta get you some of that."

Later that same day, the same staff member said to Don, "Hey, Doc. Have you met Miss Judy? Isn't she fine? She's single. You should ask her out."

However, at that time, neither of us wanted to go out on dates with someone from work since that could lead to trouble if the relationship didn't work out.

Nevertheless, after two years of working at the jail, Don asked Judy out on a date to a seafood restaurant looking out over the Atlantic Ocean.

One month later, he proposed.

Six months later, we were married!

As Judy says, "When you get to our age and have been married before, you pretty much know who you're looking for, so why waste time?!"

Judy grew up in a devout Roman Catholic family. She attended Catholic schools and was previously married in a Catholic Church.

Don grew up in a devout Protestant family. He attended public schools and was married in a (Protestant) Quaker Meeting. Judy raised her son in a Catholic parish and sent him through Catholic schools.

Don raised his two children in a Quaker congregation and sent them through Quaker schools.

Chapter 2
A Close "Call"

In July 2013, Don proposed to Judy. He felt "called" to marry Judy in the Roman Catholic tradition of Judy's family. We attended CCDC class every week.

One fine Wednesday evening at the end of class, Father Ted informed us that we would need to annul our prior marriages in order for Don to convert and for us to get married as Roman Catholics. We were astonished.

Don asked, "Father Ted, do you mean legally annulled as in signing legal papers that essentially state that I was never legally married before?"

Father Ted replied, "Yes. It's easy. You simply pay $800 in legal fees to have the paperwork completed and then sign it."

Judy frowned and said, "Are you saying that we are both going to be asked to sign a paper that says we were never legally married before?"

Father Ted replied, "The Roman Catholic Church requires this. And, there's no getting around it."

Don leaned forward, "If I were to sign a legal document like that, it would mean that I would also have to swear to God, perhaps with my hand on the Bible, that I was never married to the mother of my two children. Really?!"

Father Ted answered, "You're overthinking this. You just write a check and sign the paper."

Judy wasn't having it, so she spoke, "Father Ted, I have been a Roman Catholic all my life. Do I have to do this, too?"

Father Ted adopted a superior tone and replied, "You are divorced from the father of your son. Rome does not recognize divorce. In fact, I really should not be allowing you to take holy communion, but that's something we can overlook."

Don laughed and retorted, "Are you suggesting that if we don't annul our marriages that Judy cannot take communion anymore?!"

Father Ted looked at the floor. Then, he responded, "We can overlook it. Take a week and think about it."

Don stood up and added, "Father Ted, you're asking me to swear to God that I was never married before. And, I am sure God was present at my wedding in 1985 when I married the mother of my two children. God already knows I was married before."

Father Ted tried another argument, "Or you could say that you never loved your wife, or that you married under false pretenses."

Judy was shocked. "Are you asking me to swear on the Bible that I didn't love my husband on the day that we were married?"

Father Ted just glared.

Judy glared back, "Also, I'm not going to say I was never married before. I married my son's father in a Roman Catholic wedding, and I know God was there!"

She stood up and walked toward the door.

Don demanded, "Father Ted, where does it say all of this? Show us where we can read this."

"It's Canon law," he replied.

"Okay. So this is Church law, and not God's law," insisted Don.

"Look it up. You can read it yourself," Father Ted answered with a straight face.

Don paused, his Irish temper on low volume but high heat. "We won't be looking it up. And we won't be back. God knows who we are."

One month later, we sat in the office of Rev. Mark Bruesehoff of St. John Lutheran Church in Ocean City, NJ. We told him the sad, funny story of our "close call."

Pastor Mark smiled. He asked excellent questions about our work, our faith, and our children. He said that he would perform our wedding under the care of St. John Church.

And, on December 8, 2013, he married us in the presence of God, witnessed by 70 members of the family and friends. And, we are quite sure that God was there, too.

Conversion Immersion

We attended Lutheran services most Sundays for the next five years in Ocean City, New Jersey. However, there were a few people in that congregation during our final year there who were troublemakers. They gave in to fear about the economic viability of their Church. These very few pathetic people made Pastor Mark's ministry nearly impossible.

In May of 2019, Pastor Mark preached his last sermon at St. John Lutheran and retired from being pastor of that congregation after more than 23 years.

He is a caring and dedicated minister. His last sermon at St. John was our last church service there. He has since moved on to another Lutheran church where he is an excellent pastor.

Chapter 3

The Shoah: Holocaust Survivors and Their Families

One week after our last Sunday morning church service at St. John Lutheran, in May of 2019, Don started a new position at Jewish Family Services of Atlantic County in Margate City, New Jersey. He was the Director of a JFNA grant-funded program helping Holocaust Survivors and their families, creating and delivering PCTI-informed skills and sensitivity training for medical and social service professionals who work with and help survivors of trauma.

Jewish Family Services

Conversion Immersion

JFS is located across the street from Beth El Synagogue. Don was impressed with the brilliance, resilience, and the many successes of survivors and their children and grandchildren.

In order to better serve survivors and their families, Don enrolled in Stockton University's Master of Arts in Holocaust and Genocide Studies (MAHGS).

Gayle Rosenthal was Don's mentor. The MAHGS curriculum helped us to develop a deep appreciation of the power of hope and faith. Don was especially moved by the collection of memoirs that had been written by Holocaust survivors and their children which were shelved in the Holocaust Resource Center in the library at Stockton University such as "Once My Name was Sarah" by I. Betty Grebenschikoff, "Love with No Tomorrow: Tales of Romance During the Holocaust" by Mindelle Pierce, and "Two Voices: A Mother & Son, Holocaust Survivors" by Donald Berkman, and more than 30 others.

Sadly, in the MAHGS curriculum, Don learned about the role of Christians and others in the persecution of Jews. Especially shocking was the discovery of one of the most virulent antisemitic texts ever written, which was published nearly 500 years ago and authored by the Catholic priest Martin Luther, the founder of the protestant religion, later named for him and the namesake of the church where we were married in 2013.

In all of our years of being Roman Catholic and Lutheran, Judy and Don had never even heard of this horrific book. In fact, Adolf Hitler was so impressed with Martin Luther's book that he held it up high and in the faces of Lutheran ministers in Germany in the 1930s to advance the cause of antisemitism in the name of the nationalist fervor of the times.

History records that some Lutheran ministers refused to obey the Nazi high command and the program of antisemitism, and the ministers suffered cruel outcomes, but others joined the Nazi party. Yes, Hitler was doing his best to "make Germany great again." But that's another story.

Pastor Mark's last sermon in May of 2019 was our last day as members of that church.

Six weeks later, on a fine soft day in June of 2019, Judy asked Don, "Have you ever been to synagogue?"

And, as this story goes, we crossed the street into our new Jewish lives.

SECTION TWO

THE STORY

The first year of our Beth El Synagogue life culminates in our conversion ceremony

Chapter 4

Have you ever been to a Synagogue?

One fine day, Judy asked her husband, "Have you ever been to a synagogue?"

Don replied, "Two bar mitzvahs many years ago when I was a school teacher. And you?"

"A Jewish wedding and also a funeral years ago," she replied.

Don added, "Looks like we've got it covered."

Judy laughed and retorted, "Let's go to Beth El in Margate, right across the street from your job at JFS."

On Friday, June 28, 2019, we were greeted at the door by Cantor Ralph Goren. "Welcome," he said, and invited us in.

Minutes later, we were in the Beth El chapel with Cantor Goren, Rabbi Krauss, and a few other people. Cantor handed me a black yarmulke.

Judy asked, "May I wear one?"

"Sure, you may if you want," Gerry S. said.

Judy selected a white one from the basket near the door. Judy S. handed a blue prayer book to each of us.

Conversion Immersion

The service was led by Cantor Goren, mostly in Hebrew with beautiful melodies and harmonies. The blue prayer book had an English translation on the facing pages.

Halfway through the service, Rabbi Krauss gave a short sermon. When he finished, he said, "I see we have three couples visiting us today. Please introduce yourselves."

A man stood up and introduced himself and his wife, saying that they had driven all the way from Philadelphia that day.

"Thank you for coming such a long way to be with us."

Another man stood up, introduced himself and his wife, and said, "We are happy to be here. We are from Florida visiting family."

Rabbi smiled. "Welcome. You came a really long way. Thank you for being here."

I stood up. "We are Don and Judy Cassidy, and we drove a long way, too. We came all the way from Mays Landing."

People chuckled at my intended humor, as Mays Landing is only a 25-minute drive from Margate, New Jersey.

Rabbi Krauss responded, "Welcome. Please say your names again."

"We are Judy Cassidy and Don Cassidy."

Without missing a beat, Rabbi smiled and shifted into a thick Irish brogue as he said, "Aye, Cassidy. Now that's a fine Jewish name, it is."

We had arrived!

When davening concluded, other people introduced themselves to us and stayed awhile to get to know us and to schmooze.

As the weeks went by, Gerry and Judy S., Lorene Stopper and Ron Cruz, Judy and Jim Landau, and others made us feel welcome and included.

Whenever people ask us why we converted to Judaism, we always include in our answer that the people of our synagogue have been very important in this life-changing chapter of our journey.

Beth El Synagogue

Chapter 5

What's Old is New: We Finally Study the Bible after 60 Years

Months later, we started attending Saturday morning services in addition to Fridays. We also spent most of the afternoon on Saturdays at home reading The Torah, The Tanach, and some of the other books we purchased or were given to us by our new synagogue friends.

People told us that we didn't have to convert. We could just keep attending and participating. So, we attended week after week.

Cantor Goren explained that Jews do not recruit new members from other faiths. But many synagogues accept new members who study Torah and make a sincere commitment to living a Jewish life.

Judy replied, "I want to be Jewish."

Gerry S. asked, "You want to be Jewish?"

"Yes," Judy Cassidy replied.

"Then you already are," Gerry added.

Don asked, "Just like that?"

Judy S. smiled. "Well, there's a little more to it."

In January of 2020, we attended Rabbi Krauss's 90th birthday party and were very impressed by the choir and by some of the guest speakers, including his dear friend, Kaleem Shabazz.

Don, Rabbi Krauss, and Judy

On Sunday mornings in 2020, we also attended morning minyan. Rabbi was kind enough to stay for an additional hour every Sunday and answer our questions about our readings and Torah study.

During the COVID-19 pandemic in March through June of 2020, we asked many questions of the Rabbi and Cantor. They guided our learning in phone-based study sessions and helped us to set a date of June 7, 2020, for our formal conversion ceremony.

Prior to the pandemic, one of our favorite times of the week had been the hour or so that we would spend at Beth El in the middle of the day on Saturday. One of the main reasons we converted was Judy S's homemade soups at kiddush! We also enjoyed the conversation and singing afterward, led by Cantor Goren.

The Happy Couple

Chapter 6

COVID Shmovid

The COVID-19 pandemic was devastating to people all over the world. According to the World Health Organization, more than 7 million people died. This chapter is a tribute to all who suffered and to those who sacrificed much to help victims and their families.

Starting in late March 2020, Beth El congregation made the challenging transition from davening in the synagogue to using Zoom technology. In fact, our first experience of a Seder dinner ended up using the speaker feature on our cell phones since the brand-new Zoom technology refused to cooperate that day.

We continued to read Torah and Tanakh at home, but especially missed our time on Saturdays and Sunday mornings in the synagogue with our new friends who continued to welcome and include us.

Every morning, we watched the TV news broadcasts of the coverage of the worldwide COVID-19 outbreak. We prayed for guidance on what we might do to keep ourselves safe and to help those who were suffering.

Judy was in her final year of graduate studies and struggled to find internship sites and supervisors to guide her practicums. Fortunately, Dr. Norm Chazin, Dr. Momodu, and others provided valuable experiences and guidance.

Conversion Immersion

There's an old saying: "Watch out what you pray for . . . you might get it." And that's what happened to Don.

During the summer of 2020, we were praying daily and asking what we could do to help people suffering from the deadly spread of COVID-19.

The phone rang one week later. It wasn't God . . . not directly. A human resources recruiter asked me if I would work full-time as a psychologist in skilled nursing facilities, also known as "nursing homes."

So, this was the answer to our prayers? Yes. I worked full-time helping people who were sad, scared, depressed, manic, and otherwise in need of a psychologist and a Jewish Irish storyteller who dared to put on layers of plastic over professional clothes, a lab coat, and a yarmulke.

Often, people simply needed to have a trained listener as they vented their fears and lamented being disconnected from family and friends who were not even allowed to visit these buildings in the early days of the pandemic.

I found ways of delivering psychological services while also allowing people of many faith traditions to pray for healing, and brought copies of The Tanach (the Hebrew Bible), the Christian Bible, and the Quran to people. I bought a kufi for a man who wanted to pray five times a day in his room at the nursing home and said that having a kufi would help him pray to Allah every day.

Conversion Immersion

Chessed and tikkum olam became part of my daily practice as a mental health professional. Years prior, as a Quaker psychologist, I looked for the inner light to help people heal. One of my Jewish clients explained to me that now I would be calling that same light "neshama."

Chapter 7

Jewish Connection: The Power of We

One month before our conversion on June 7, 2020, we suggested that Beth El have a weekly group discussion using the Zoom format. All of us missed our weekly conversations during kiddush on Saturdays. Cantor Goren suggested that we have this Zoom-based event on Saturday evenings after Shabbat ended.

Fortunately, most people were able to use the Zoom link to sign on to this new weekly event, which we named "Jewish Connection." The first meeting occurred on May 23, 2020, and it wasn't long before we had 15 to 20 people joining us each week for an hour of storytelling and Jewish schmoozing.

The first meeting focused on the topic, "Why Be Jewish?" Group members offered a variety of answers and told wonderful stories from their lives. We were surprised to find out how many other members of Beth El were converts just like we now were.

Five years later now, at the time of the publishing of this book, Cantor Goren has continued as the Zoom host, and Judy and Don have served as discussion leaders of topics that entertain us, inform us, and also facilitate our being connected with each other.

Conversion Immersion

Jewish Connection was especially important during the COVID-19 pandemic when nearly all synagogue activities were held over the internet.

However, in the year 2025, now that the worst of the pandemic has subsided, Jewish Connection continues to meet most Saturday nights with 12 - 20 people showing up for topics such as these: "Have you ever had an experience when you were touched by the hand of God?"; "Laughter is the Best Medicine"; "Life is a Beach Travel Stories"; "How do each of us celebrate Chanukkah?"; "Languages Connect Us: Each one teach one"; "Music and Arts Night"; "Favorite Jewish Dishes'; "Ask the Rabbi" and many other wonderful topics.

Chapter 8

Taking the Plunge: Conversion Day

On Sunday, June 7, 2020, we wore our finest clothes, including new yarmulkes and talis we had recently purchased at Beth El Synagogue gift shop. We gathered in the library for our conversion ceremony with Rabbi Krauss and Cantor Goren officiating. Gerry S. and Judy S. also spoke, asked questions, and served as our witnesses. We had been studying nearly every day for the past year to prepare.

We then walked to a building which housed a mikvah. Don took the plunge first, witnessed by Cantor Goren. Then Judy entered the mikvah for her ceremony, witnessed by Judy S.

Judy Cassidy remembers singing the Shemah in full voice with deep emotions. Our Jewish lives and bodies felt new. And now, we were no longer simply "wet behind the ears," we were converted and immersed from head to toe!

We walked back to Beth El, and we all signed our certificate under the care of Rabbi Krauss and Cantor Goren.

We drove home to Mays Landing and took pictures on our front porch with our Magen David stars on the doors behind us. *A new day. A new dawn.* We were now praying to the same God we had known all of our lives, but we now address God as "Hashem" and "Adonai," and our lives continue to be blessed.

Each morning we awake and call out, "Modeh Ani."

Hashem answers, "Are yous good?"

(God says "yous" because God's from Philly. We know God is also from other places, too, but speaks to us with words we understand.)

"Yeah. We're good. Thank you for another day."

"No worries," Hashem replies. "Now go to work. Be my eyes, and ears, and hands, and voice. I can't do it all."

Don makes coffee for Judy. After her second cup, she makes breakfast for both of us. Then, we go and do the work Hashem blesses us to do.

SECTION THREE
THE EMERGING STORY

Humorous and provocative stories show how our conversion leads us deeper into chessed, simcha, and ashrei. But, also, we are now asked disturbing questions by friends and relatives

Chapter 9

The Jesus Questions, or a Funny Thing Happened on Our Way to Salvation

People ask us the most amazing questions. You wouldn't believe.

"Have you forgotten about Jesus as your personal Savior?"

"Aren't you afraid you'll go to Hell when you die?"

And, my favorite question, "What do you mean that you talked to God this morning?"

Before we converted, we had it made! What were we thinking? We were both baptized, confirmed, took communion, and had accepted Jesus as our Savior at a young age ... the true Messiah ... the one and only path to salvation and eternal life in Heaven. How could we give up a sure thing? That would be like throwing away a winning lottery ticket.

Nevertheless, we have wondered what happened to all of the poor souls who were born hundreds and thousands of years before Jesus died on the cross. How did all of those folks get to Heaven since they had died without being baptized or having accepted Jesus as their savior? You see, we have questions of our own.

At the ages of 65 and 67, we were all set ... we could have retired from our day jobs. We could have lived out our lives as the good

Christians we had become. And, we didn't need to do any more good deeds … we didn't need to heal the world or anyone in it. We didn't need to follow the 'golden rule' of doing unto others as we would have them do unto us.

All we needed to do was to accept Jesus, even if at the last minute, even if our sins vastly outweighed our good deeds, even if our name was "Hitler", God forbid, and we would go to Heaven when we died. Such a deal.

Why would we trade in our chance to meet St. Peter at Heaven's gate … and for what? To become Jewish? Who does that?

What does Judaism offer if it doesn't believe in Heaven? What is this "Olam Haba" all about? Where is it? Who will be there after we die? Is Moses standing there next to St. Peter at the gate of Heaven? Is there a gate at Olam Haba? Oy vey, such questions.

As it turns out, we converted to Judaism because we chose to be Jewish. We hope that Jesus will really be in Heaven to greet us and not just St. Peter and Moses. We have many questions for all three of them.

However, and it's a pretty big "however," we hadn't thought very much about our friends and relatives who might be afraid that we would end up in Hell, and miss out on salvation. Some of our friends and relatives are agnostics or atheists, so they're not worried about us. We regret any angst that our conversion may cause anyone.

Conversion Immersion

With no disrespect intended to our Christian and Muslim friends and family members, neither one of us can remember actually believing in Hell, even when we were kids. Well, maybe when I was only 7 years old, but not for long did I worry about the Hell my Sunday school teacher tried to teach us. So, neither one of us was giving up a cherished belief on the Salvation issue.

Jesus of Nazareth is an inspiration for many. A man of God. Jesus was a rabbi in that he was a teacher who healed the sick and ministered to the poor. Jesus delivered powerful sermons with powerful messages, and his holy spirit still performs miracles every day.

We have not "left Jesus behind" as some suggest. We live our lives following his example of tikkun olam, "healing the world."

Jesus was not the founder of Christianity. Another famous Jew named Saul, later called Paul, was actually the founder of Christianity. Given the atrocities which have been committed in the name of Christian zeal, like the Crusades and the Spanish Inquisition, even Jesus himself is probably not all that excited about a religion named after him which does not always seem to follow the 'golden rule' when it comes to people who don't look like or pray like "a good Christian."

And, it was NOT the Jews who murdered Jesus. The Romans killed Jesus because they were afraid of his power, and of his excellent example, and that people might follow him instead of paying tribute to Cesar.

Famously and ironically, Jesus was okay with the Romans up to a point. He preached that his followers should give to the Romans what they asked. "Render unto Caesar that which is Caesar's. Give unto God that which is God's."

Yes. A funny thing did happen on the way to salvation. We converted to the religion that is the foundation and the roots of Christianity, and also eventually Islam.

Who does that? We did, and we do it again each new day that God wakes us up and blesses us with the opportunity to be his eyes and ears and hands and voice as we allow God's love to work through us.

Christians and Muslims do the same as we do. They follow the 10 Commandments and do God's work every day, even though their name for God might be Jesus or Allah.

During our first year of intense study of the Torah and Tanach, we were told that we did not need to convert to Judaism to continue to be active and to participate in synagogue life.

"We don't actively recruit people to convert. It's a big commitment," Cantor Goren and others told us.

We replied that we were aware that there is much to learn and to consider. However, neither one of us was ever afraid of hard work as long as it was the right thing to do.

Conversion Immersion

(Author's note: We respect all religions and traditions. The somewhat humorous tone of this chapter is NOT meant to disrespect any human being or any religion. Laughter is the best medicine and heals many of our anxieties and sad times. If this chapter allows you to laugh along with us, that is good. If this chapter does not amuse you at all, we apologize. We do not suggest that our opinions and experiences are correct or right for you. We merely present our story as our experience. We hope you enjoy it.)

Chapter 10

Top Ten Reasons We Converted

1. The Clergy: Rabbi Krauss and Cantor Goren . . . a Jewish dynamic duo.

2. The Congregation: Beth El is a hamisch shul: "Jews by Choice Choose Beth El."

3. The Tanach: We read the Torah, then the entire Tanach.

4. Jewish Music!!! Synagogue melodies and harmonies, The Maccabeats, The Beth El Choir, Debbie Friedman, Shimi Goodman, and more!!

5. The Jewish Holidays.

6. The Sermon: "Accept, Forgive, Love" ... One good wedding sermon deserves another.

7. Chessed, Mitzvot, and Tikkun Olam: These breathe through us every day.

8. Our Jewish Wedding: Mazel Tov!

9. Lifelong Learning: A Jewish Way of Living.

10. Our work in the mental health field is especially strengthened by our Jewish faith and practice.

Chapter 11

Rabbi Aaron Krauss

(A man who sat next to Golda Meir and marched with Martin Luther King, Jr., and is a new friend to many people he meets.)

Some day, someone will write the impressive story of Rabbi Aaron Krauss's life and profound impact on the people who have the privilege of knowing him. Today is not that day.

Instead of listing his accomplishments, we have devoted this chapter to how Rabbi has touched our lives since we first met him in the year 2019.

Rabbi Aaron Krauss is our mentor and treasured leader of our synagogue. We value his kindness, vision, storytelling, Torah scholarship, intelligence, and his humor. We especially value his outreach beyond the four walls of our synagogue to the greater interfaith and diverse Atlantic County, New Jersey community.

One day in 2023, Don exclaimed, "Hey, look at this!"

The front page story of The Press of Atlantic City featured an article about three outstanding civic leaders who have contributed much to interfaith initiatives and activities in the Atlantic City area.

Rabbi Krauss is quoted in the article: "I was called the Black rabbi. Jewish and non-Jewish people criticized me." He is also quoted as saying that being Jewish "is not determined by skin tone."

Starting back in the 1960s when he met and marched with Martin Luther King, Jr., Rabbi Krauss originated and promoted initiatives to create alliances with Muslim and Christian congregations. He continues to be an influence in helping Beth El to grow in its commitment to egalitarian issues and practices with regard to the roles of men and women in synagogue life. He inspires us.

The Bridge of Faith

The Press of Atlantic City published a feature article on the front page of the February 9, 2023 edition with the headline "Interfaith Alliance: Jews, Blacks worked together over the years to improve A. C."

Conversion Immersion

An impressive photo of Rabbi Krauss, Kaleem Shabazz and Rev. Collins Davis accompanies the description of the multicultural and interfaith coalition which has had several names over the years. These three leaders have built an alliance of Muslims, Jews, and Christians who are connected by their shared commitment to community service, civil rights, and good deeds in our communities and in the world.

Neither of us knew much about the long history of Gentiles and Jews and how we are, and can be, very much a part of each other's lives. Rabbi Krauss was a significant person in the renaming of one of the streets in Margate, New Jersey, in honor of Raoul Wallenburg, who was a righteous gentile who launched a rescue operation of Jews in Hungary during the 1940s, providing passports and shelter during the Holocaust.

As Gentiles by birth, we were initially shy about feeling welcome and included in our Jewish community. We did not even know, until more recently, that there are Jewish people literally all over the world of every ethnicity, skin color, and culture.

Rabbi Krauss continually reminds all of us about these facts through his delightful stories.

For us, Rabbi Krauss is not only the religious and spiritual leader of our synagogue. He officiated at our conversion in 2020, he performed our Jewish wedding ceremony in February 2022, our B'nai Mitzvah in 2025, and continues to make our Torah learning rich and full.

Conversion Immersion

More recently, two of our four grandsons were visiting us when the synagogue featured a brief celebration of Rabbi's 94th birthday on the Zoom-based Jewish Connection. Our grandson, Clark, called out, "Happy Birthday, Rabbi!" and grandson Jack blew a kiss to Rabbi, who answered, "Oooh. Thank you, boys. Thank you!"

Rabbi Krauss is full of surprises. For my 70th birthday, we invited more than 50 people to celebrate with a big party in the social hall at Beth El. Ten people were invited to be guest speakers, and Rabbi started it off by taking the stage wearing the Irish cap that Judy and I had given him for his 90th birthday years ago! As usual, his words were spiritual, humorous, and filled with wisdom.

Another example of his wit came on the occasion of our Jewish wedding in February 2022. We had asked our son, Jude, to serve as the 'best man', as our other son, Kyle, and daughter, Meghan, were in Maryland in COVID quarantine.

As the wedding ceremony was about to begin on the bima, Rabbi asked everyone in the wedding party to introduce themselves. When it was Jude's turn to introduce himself, Rabbi replied, "Oh! With that beard, you look like a rabbi."

During my four years working at Stockton University, I was completely unaware of Rabbi Krauss's role in the founding of the college back in the late 1960s.

As the story goes, Stockton University, back then Richard Stockton State College, might not have ever happened without the efforts and impassioned advocacy of our dear Rabbi, meeting with the New Jersey State governor and explaining why having a state college in South Jersey, in Atlantic County, was a very good idea.

After much convincing and advocacy, the Governor was able to move legislation through the New Jersey State Assembly. He then called Rabbi on the telephone and said, "Rabbi, you've got your college."

Judy and I attended his 90th birthday party in 2020, and also attended his 95th birthday celebration in 2025. At the end of the party, I said, "Happy Birthday, young man. Now we are looking forward to your 100th birthday celebration."

He smiled, "I'll see what I can do!"

I replied, "Good, because Judy and I are going to be on the planning committee for that celebration five years from now."

Rabbi replied with a chuckle, "The Age of Miracles has not yet ended!"

Chapter 12

Rabbi Jonathan Sacks (of blessed memory)

The most powerful mentor we never met

Very sadly, he died in November 2020, not long after we had first "met" him through his work broadcast over the internet. He was a living presence due to our readings of his many books, and also watching countless lectures, TED talks, and various other messages which are broadcast over YouTube and the Rabbi Sacks website.

His recorded message, entitled "Why I am a Jew," is powerful and impressive. Our DJ broadcast it over the sound system at the beginning of our Jewish wedding reception in February of 2022.

The following is a list of some of his books on our bookshelves at home.

BOOKS: (a few of the 30+ books):

1. A Letter in the Scroll
2. Morality
3. Lessons in Leadership
4. The Power of Ideas
5. Studies in Spirituality

YouTube Presentations. There is a seemingly endless supply of free video presentations, many of which are lectures and presentations. Here is a selection of some of our favorites.

1. Desert Island Texts
2. How to live a good life in divided times
3. A Tale of Two Women (Ruth and Naomi)
4. Happiness in the Jewish perspective.
5. Investing Time

10 Life Changing Principles:

1. Give thanks.
2. Give children values, not presents.
3. Be a lifelong learner.
4. Never compromise your Judaism in public.
5. Forgive.
6. Do not talk evil speech.
7. Keep Shabbat holy.
8. Volunteer.
9. Create moments of joy every day.
10. And, most importantly … Love. Love God. Love your neighbor as you love yourself.

Rabbi Sacks is a profound influence on human beings of all faiths, cultures, and nationalities. He will probably always be the most powerful mentor that we have never met. His work continues to be carried on through the Rabbi Sacks organization.

Learn more at RabbiSacks.org

Chapter 13

The Maccabeats: An extraordinary all-male Jewish a cappella singing group

Music is both figure and ground in Jewish life. Religious and secular, vocal and instrumental, traditional and modern, we celebrate God, and thus we celebrate life through music.

The Maccabeats are an American Orthodox Jewish all-male a cappella singing group founded in 2007 at Yeshiva University in New York. The 14+ member group specializes in covers and parodies of contemporary hits using Jewish-themed lyrics. They are hugely successful, but they are much more than that. They are courageous! They tour worldwide and have performed at the White House and the Knesset.

Before the year 2019, we knew nothing of this delightful performance group. For more than five years, we have listened to many of their songs and even have many songs memorized simply by listening to them so often. We are moved by their messages and by their brilliant harmonies, beats, rhythms, and musicianship.

We were fortunate to attend a concert on Dec. 8, 2024, at the Performing Arts Center of Stockton University on our 11th wedding anniversary! They also offered one song without microphones... as if in a synagogue.

Breathtaking.

Their courage, their music, and their message … role models for new hope for our troubled times … the next generation… beyond faith identity… reaching out to people of all Faith traditions.

After the concert at the signature table in the P.A.C. lobby, I mentioned to them that they are one of the "top ten" reasons we converted!

Their leader asked, "What're the other nine?"

And, I replied, "We will send you our book, and you can read about it!" Without missing a beat, they sang "Happy Anniversary to You" in 4-part harmony!!

"Words are the language of the mind. Music is the language of the soul." -Rabbi Sacks.

Chapter 14

Mildred Krauss (of blessed memory): A Matter of Life and Death

We met Millie Krauss at Beth El Synagogue on a number of occasions, including Saturday mornings, sitting in her traditional place off to the right as we looked toward the bima. She always greeted us with great kindness. Because we started attending in 2019, we did not have the privilege of knowing her in her many active roles in the synagogue, such as a Hebrew school teacher.

Over the years, she would sometimes attend Jewish Connection via the Zoom link, standing beside Rabbi. Invariably, people in the JC Zoom group would call out, "Hi, Millie," and she would always smile and wave to us.

Her life ended as it had begun... on Shabbat. February 10, 2024, was a sad day for all of us: it was announced that she had passed away peacefully in her sleep earlier that morning.

As the words "standing beside Rabbi Krauss" appear above on this page, we are reminded of several speakers at her funeral who spoke not only of her life as a mother and as a teacher, but also as the wife who stood beside Rabbi in their family life and in synagogue life.

On July 4, 2025, we had the honor to attend the unveiling at the cemetery. Cantor Goren conducted the ceremony at the graveside, which was attended by children, grandchildren, and dear friends who came to honor her.

Rabbi spoke the most beautiful words, told stories about their wedding, their honeymoon, and how much he misses her every single day. We felt so honored to attend this heartbreakingly beautiful gathering at the Beth Kehillah Cemetery.

Millie earned a BA from Newark State Teachers College and an MA from Seton Hall University. She then taught elementary school until marrying Rabbi Krauss. After all her children were grown, Millie resumed her career as a teacher at the Hebrew Academy, where she was a beloved teacher of Hebrew, English, and cooking. She was devoted to her family and her faith, and we are honored to have known her.

Chapter 15

Our Lionel Train Platform Converts!

Ten years ago, we created a Lionel train set, including David Winter houses, villages, and a landscape in our living room. The train platform featured a 6-foot-tall Christmas tree decorated for the December holidays.

One night, right after our conversion ceremony, Don awoke from a dream that the train platform had a Noah's ark with animals, a synagogue, and a village which resembled Anatevke from Fiddler on the Roof. Over the years, the train set has doubled in size and experienced its own conversion!

Our Lionel Train Platform Converts

One of the villages is Margate City, NJ, and it even has its own Lucy the Elephant, purchased from their gift shop. A mountain resort hotel represents The Catskills.

Visiting neighbors and grandchildren experience the train landscape as a play set. This is NOT a fancy display with signs that say "do not touch." Quite the country, the buildings and animals and even the train cars themselves get rearranged and played with by young hands and inquiring minds. When something breaks, it is fixed or replaced, just like the real world . . . Tikkun olam . . . heal the world.

We hope that someday children might be able to identify Noah's Ark, Mt. Sinai, Jerusalem, Persia, Egypt, Ethiopia, Poland, Anatevka, Margate, Vineland, and the Irish village.

As they play, we hope they are learning that our Jewish story is alive and real and not something that we simply read about in a book.

Chapter 16

A Sad Thing Happened on Our Way to the Holy Land: October 7, 2023

We went on a vacation cruise to the Mediterranean, October 15 - 26, 2023, on the Regent Seven Seas Voyager. The main attraction was to have been the opportunity to fly to Tel Aviv and spend three days in Israel and two days in Egypt. Most of the passengers on this cruise selected this particular vacation for exactly the same reason. This would have been our first trip to the Holy Land.

However, a war started in Israel on October 7th, exactly one week prior to our intended plane flight to Tel Aviv. Our travel was diverted, and the cruise took us to Turkey, Greece, and Italy. The war that ensued has cost tens of thousands of civilian lives and is a tragic chapter in the history of human beings on both sides of the conflict.

We had a good enough time on the cruise, but it was hard to enjoy ourselves knowing what was happening a thousand miles to the south.

Vacation cruise lines sometimes provide what is needed in order to have a Friday evening Shabbat service. Regent Cruise staff provided kosher wine, challah, and prayer booklets for the Shabbat service on Friday, October 20th.

Conversion Immersion

Shabbat services are offered every Friday night on some cruises, and a suitable location was allocated on the top deck of the ship in a dining area. As usual, the service was conducted by a knowledgeable Jewish passenger.

As it turned out, one of the featured entertainers on this cruise was an Israeli man named Shimi Goodman, an internationally-acclaimed operatic tenor. He conducted a beautiful Shabbat service. Shimi performs a wide range of music internationally with a powerful and emotional style. Judy and I encourage the readers of this section of our story to put his name into an internet search to view his website.

Shimi Goodman also told us the story of his day on October 7th. He was in Tel Aviv to give a concert with pianist Christopher Hamilton that day. They were just barely able to get out of the country and joined the Regent cruise a week later. Shimi and Christopher gave a special presentation regarding their experiences and signed copies of their music CD.

We felt honored to be in their presence.

Chapter 17

Antisemitism: A Mutating Virus

"Antisemitism starts with Jews, but it never ends with Jews." Rabbi Sacks wrote and spoke powerfully that antisemitism is a virus that mutates over the centuries. One of his best works on this topic is his book entitled "Not in God's Name."

During his nearly 50 years as a rabbi, Chief Rabbi Sacks devoted significant time and effort to bringing people of all faiths, traditions, and even people who call themselves atheists together in efforts for local and world peace. He helped students in England to develop a program where Jewish students lead the fight against Islamaphobia, and Muslim students lead the efforts against antisemitism in England. He was a rabbi who talked the talk, but he also powerfully walked the walk.

In our work as mental health professionals, we encounter antisemitic remarks. Don dealt with an ethnic slur from an ignorant man by being unexpectedly kind to him. This was the exact opposite of what the man expected, and his fear-based epithet did not repeat itself. Don's kindness disarmed the man's ignorance and fear.

Judy was just doing her job one day, appropriately refusing to prescribe a particular medication to an angry young man, plagued by his addiction process.

His anger got the best of him as he said loudly, "Give me my script, you f-ing Jew!"

The office manager at this particular job site explained to him that it was time for him to leave the building.

So far, these incidents have been the exception. Mostly, people are fascinated by our Jewish faith and practice. Sometimes, Don has the opportunity to tell an abbreviated version of our having converted from Christianity to Judaism.

At the end of these brief stories, the listener often says, "Hey! You've gotta write this story."

So, here it is.

Chapter 18

Our Jewish Wedding: Mazel Tov!

On February 20, 2022, Rabbi Krauss married us under a beautiful chuppah as we exchanged our vows and plain gold wedding bands in our new faith tradition. Rabbi's message to us was wise, strong, and filled with hope for our future as a Jewish couple. Despite a new wave of COVID, more than 50 people attended and celebrated our wedding with songs by Cantor Goren, Denise, and Tammy.

The Beautiful Chuppah

Our wedding reception featured Kosher catering by Gila, hora dancing, and group photos of our relatives and also our Beth El family.

As we sat down at our table, the DJ played an audio recording of "Why I am a Jew" by Rabbi Sacks, which gave voice to our own reasons for being Jews. The words are available on the Rabbi Sacks website.

The Hora Dance

One of the delights at our reception was the "surprise" appearance of a group of dancers in black coats and hats who reenacted the bottle dance from the wedding scene of Fiddler on the Roof.

Wedding Reception Bottle Dancers

The comedy of the moment was heightened by the appearance of an actor pretending to be a rabbi who showed up "by mistake" at our synagogue looking for a bar mitzvah party.

The "Amazing Bottle Dancers", the invention of Michael Pasternak, who created the event more than 20 years ago for his own wedding reception! Now, his talented dancers are available for hire at special events like weddings, bar mitzvahs, bat mitzvahs, and other celebrations and simchas. We enjoyed their performance so much that Don hired them again to appear at his 70th birthday party.

Wedding Reception Bottle Dancers

Chapter 19

I Married a Jewish Doctor

Five days a week, we both put on a white lab jacket and go to work. Don is a psychologist who works every day in skilled nursing facilities, helping people to manage their anxiety, depression, sadness, psychosis, addictions, and loneliness. Judy works every day as a psychiatric mental health nurse practitioner.

In this role, she functions in the exact same way that psychiatrists do, prescribing medicine for people who suffer from anxiety, depression, psychotic disorders, and addictions. As Jews, we are doing the work that Hashem wants us to do, helping people who really need our help … healing the world one person at a time.

Don has worked in the field of education, one way or another, for more than 50 years. He agrees with the following statement, which Rabbi Sacks once wrote, "Those who can, do. Those who can't … teach. And, teaching is the higher calling."

For the two of us, our work as mental health professionals includes both teaching and healing. We are living the legacy of Rabbi Sacks because our work every day is a "calling."

At our age, we certainly could retire and spend more time visiting family, traveling the world, and living the busy lives that many retirees live.

On the day he turned 70, Don announced that he had definitely set his retirement date, which would be in about 15 years, when he turns 85! By then, of course, he won't be driving all over South Jersey working in skilled nursing facilities, as we plan to further develop our private practice using telepsychology and telepsychiatry, so that we can work many days from our offices in our home.

Residents of nursing homes ask Don why he wears a yarmulke with a name like Cassidy, which is famously an Irish name.

"Are you Jewish?"

Don has several replies to this question: "Yes ... Cassidy ... my rabbi assured us that Cassidy is a fine Jewish name!"

Or, even more fun is this: "Oh, yes. You want to know if there are any Jews in Ireland. Is that right? Wow, yes, there are Jews in Ireland. In fact, I know all 10 of them!" Then Don explains that there are synagogues and Chabads in Ireland, and that at least one mayor of Dublin has been Jewish.

Judy wears a Magen David (Star of David) necklace and other jewelry to work and has mostly received compliments and best wishes around Jewish holiday times.

As a psychiatric mental health nurse practitioner, Judy does the same work that a psychiatrist does, helping patients with their psychiatric medication and offering gentle counsel and advice.

Due to her role and her white lab coat, patients sometimes call her "Dr. Cassidy." Meanwhile, in his role as a clinical psychologist, Don is addressed as "Dr. Cassidy" in work settings.

Neither one of us previously thought that one day we would marry a Jewish doctor!

Chapter 20

Our Wellness Private Practice Converts: "Coast to Coast Counseling, LLC" becomes "Ashrei Wellness Services, LLC"

Donald Cassidy, PhD, and Judith Cassidy, PMHNP-BC, have a private practice called "Ashrei Wellness Services, LLC," where we help people with many of the issues and problems that challenge all of us.

Ten years ago, our practice was named "Coast to Coast Counseling, LLC," but we changed the name to signal that we have a strong spiritual basis to the work we do, and that the goal for many people when they come to therapy is to achieve wellness and happiness. That is the essence of ashrei, a Hebrew word that means happiness.

In our work as mental health professionals, we know that we earn a good living, which allows us to live comfortably, and to give money to our families, our synagogue, and to charitable causes in the USA and also in other places in the world.

The Hebrew words "tikkun olam" translate in English to "repair the world." We may not be healing the world, because it seems that every day, the local news, the national news, and the world news suggest otherwise. But maybe we are helping to heal the world one person at a time.

Judy prescribes psychiatric medication and kindness. Don prescribes Irish humor, storytelling/listening, balancing, generosity, and therapy to help people balance and reconnect.

Moses is considered to be a prophet by Jews, Christians, and Muslims. Among other lessons which Moses taught all of us is that we are God's eyes and ears, and we do God's work through our voices and our hands.

Please look us up on our website: www.ashreiwellness.com

Chapter 21

Wondering Jews: We Wonder as We Wander

We have attended synagogue services and prayer services in New Jersey, New York, Hawaii, Puerto Rico, Delaware, on a cruise ship in the Mediterranean, and in Rome, Italy. Congregations at Orthodox, Conservative, and Reform shuls all welcome our attendance.

The Friday evening Shabbat service on a cruise ship in the Mediterranean had nearly 40 Jews and also had non-Jews in attendance and prayer. We also attended a Shabbat service on a different cruise ship in the Caribbean that had a small number of people, and Judy and I found ourselves helping another couple to conduct the service. That was an unexpected honor.

Jews in Ireland? Hawaii? Who knew? Our travels remind us that Jews are everywhere.

Meeting and making new Jewish friends has been an unforgettable pleasure: Marty and Lois from California, Harriet and Paul from Georgia, Arthur and Fran Beckerman from California, and Sandra and Don from Hawaii have made us feel welcome as we find ourselves being strangers in strange lands.

In fact, we were further inspired to publish this book when we visited Hawaii and were gifted a copy of "A Jewish Girl and a Not-So-Jewish Boy," written by Sandra Armstrong. Their story of her husband's conversion to Judaism is a delightful read.

In February of 2024, we attended a Shabbat service at Central Synagogue in New York City. We were welcomed by everyone during the service and at the meal afterwards. We did not know it at the time, but we might have been there at the same time as my Swarthmore College friend, Andrew Miller and his family! Our time there was so overwhelmingly positive that we certainly would have converted to Judaism if we had not done so at our own Beth El!

In May 2025, Judy and I celebrated my 50th college reunion of the class of 1975 of Swarthmore College. Sitting around the dining hall, we casually shared our stories, and many were surprised to hear me talk with great excitement about the upcoming B'nai Mitzvah that Judy and I planned to celebrate in November 2025. And imagine my surprise that many of my classmates attending the reunion are Jewish. The last time I was at Swarthmore, I was a Lutheran who became a Quaker. Now, Sam Agger, Andrew Miller, and others sitting at our lunch and dinner tables were fascinated with our story and wanted to know the exact date of our celebration in November.

We wonder as we wander where we will daven next ...

Chapter 22

A Chosen People: Are Jews "the" chosen people, or "a" chosen people?

We want to offer a humble and emerging opinion to this controversial and timeless question that we are "a" chosen people.

This is sometimes described as one of the most difficult Faith questions to discuss. We believe that Jews are "one" of the chosen peoples. This puts us at odds with others who believe that Jews are "the" chosen people.

More than 800 years ago, Moses Maimonides wrote important letters to converts. His letter to a man named Ovadiah reassured him that he was fully Jewish, and was even greater than a born Jew because his lineage traced to God Himself, not just Abraham.

Someday, I hope to write an entire short pamphlet on the subject of "choice" and being "chosen". At the time of this writing in 2025, however, less is more.

Chapter 23
Dr. Cantor Rabbi Ralph Goren

Cantor Goren is our mentor and synagogue friend. He always does his utmost to help everyone and is an excellent cantor and choir leader. He is an ordained rabbi and also recently received an honorary doctorate. He has tirelessly kept services going, and even done so at times when he was exhausted by the COVID-19 virus.

Cantor Ralph has volunteered his musical abilities at the JCC, at Devotion by the Ocean beach services, and also entertains us during the Jewish Connection group. On the occasion of his 19th anniversary of being the Cantor of our synagogue several years ago, he gave a Zoom-based concert entitled "Cantor-19," which honored not only his 19 years of service at Beth El at the time but also his ironic sense of humor, as this concert had to be given on Zoom format due to the COVID-19 pandemic.

Cantor has been a mentor since the very first day we walked in the door. In an unexpected twist of fate, it turns out that one of Judy's bichon dogs was a relative of Cantor's dog, Moti of blessed memory. Cantor had purchased Moti many years ago from Judy's sister, Maryjane, who was a bichon breeder.

We even had a puppy play day at our house when Moti came to run around with our dog, Spotty. Many times, Spotty perked up and tilted his head to one side whenever he heard Cantor's voice during Zoom events like Jewish Connection on Saturday nights. It seems that Cantor and Spotty had a bichon connection!

Don, Rabbi Krauss, Judy, Cantor Goren

Chapter 24

Shared Leadership: A Jewish Way of Life

Many people at Beth El Synagogue fulfill and share leadership roles. This way of davening and conducting the business of synagogue community life is quintessentially Jewish. Other communities of faith also share leadership. Jews share leadership because our role models in the Torah and the Tanach have shown us for more than 3,000 years that this is how we survive and thrive.

We suggest that everyone read LESSONS IN LEADERSHIP: A weekly reading of the Jewish Bible by Rabbi Jonathan Sacks. Each chapter features a week in the Jewish calendar and presents the story of a Jewish leader and what made their leadership matter to us: Abraham, Sarah, Noah, Esther, Isaac, Rebecca, Moses, Ruth, and dozens of other men and women who lived their own stories of leading people.

Most stories of Jewish leadership emphasize what Rabbi Sacks describes as "the power of ideas over the idea of power." Beth El has many leaders sharing many roles: Rabbi, Cantor, Trustees, Hadassah Presidents, Jewish Connection facilitators, Choir members, Torah carriers, Shofar sounders, Hebrew School teachers, kiddush cooks, and many other roles.

Chapter 25

Our Jewish "Godparents"

Gerry and Judy S have always "been there for us" since our arrival. They gave us some of the books we needed to get started. They listened as we asked their counsel and advice.

When we purchased a memorial stained glass panel to honor our fathers, it was Gerry who made sure that it was installed in the synagogue in good order. We called each other on the phone from time to time to keep in touch during these unprecedented COVID times. They were especially helpful when Don was first diagnosed with esophageal cancer, offering home remedies to add to our medical procedures. Every synagogue would do well to establish "godparents" for people who convert.

Gerry and Judy S. are very humble people, and probably wish we had not written this chapter! So, that's all we have to say about that …

Chapter 26
Synagogue Family and Friends

We will never get tired of hearing the phrase "welcome to the family." This expression of connection in a faith family is not unique to Judaism.

Howard and Jill Slotoroff (of blessed memory) invited us to their home many times, where we shared stories of our families and delicious food. Jill is an accomplished artist who created the cover art for this book. Her artwork ranges from portraits to delicate crafts of breathtaking beauty. Her art and craft emerged from her deep, spiritual vision and from her dreams.

Howard is a renowned surgeon and doctor. He has also owned and trained successful champion trotting horses.

Norm Chazin has been a colleague and friend ever since we met him at Stockton University in 2015. He has been a professional mentor. He tells us that at one point in his life, he was married at the Beth El Synagogue with Rabbi Aaron Krauss. We are fans of the Philadelphia Eagles and were at his house when the Eagles won the Super Bowl in 2018. Also, Norm was at our house for dinner and said the blessing of the challah before Shabbat dinner.

Tammy and Lee S. invited us, and other recent Beth El converts, for dinner at their house. Tammy has helped many of us recently in our conversion process and is our Hebrew teacher. She cooked a delicious, organic, kosher dinner. The evening flew by, and we felt more connected with each other, and Lee told wonderful stories.

Denise Borisch has been a mentor for us on too many topics to write here. Suffice it to say she has helped both of us with many projects, including the Fathers Memorial Fund, blessing and cutting the challah at our wedding, and many other ways she has blessed us with her friendship.

Chapter 27

Hadassah Women's Group

In 2020, we felt honored to be accepted into the Golda Meir chapter of the international Hadassah organization. We have attended luncheon meetings led by Denise. We also have enjoyed business meetings and social activities such as the group theatre trips. Hadassah at Beth El had two groups, one led by Tammy and the other by Denise, and has recently consolidated under new leadership and continues to be involved in local and world activities.

During one luncheon meeting at The Shore Diner, as the meeting was ending, Jill Slotoroff introduced herself to Judy. This was the start of a great friendship.

Chapter 28

Melvin Gregory: "I'm a Sabbath-keeper."

Don had the good fortune of learning from many mentors during his four years working at Stockton University, including Mel Gregory.

Mel has been a colleague and friend of ours for nearly 10 years now. Judy and Don were walking across a parking lot on their way to a fitness gym. On this occasion, we were singing a duet which we intended to perform later that evening at a karaoke event. As we approached the front door, we heard a strong, cheerful voice call out to us, "Is that The Captain and Tennille?"

Without missing a beat, Don replied to this perfect stranger, "No, it's Sonny and Cher!" That meeting was the beginning of a strong friendship that has lasted until this day, including several wonderful new chapters at Beth El Synagogue.

In 2015, Mel was helpful to Don by alerting him that a job position had opened up for the Director of Counseling at the Wellness Center at Stockton University. He also assisted Judy as she pursued admission to Stockton University for her BSN studies.

Don and Mel collaborated on many occasions, helping Stockton University undergraduates who had special learning needs. When Mel finally retired from Stockton, that could have been the end of our story. However, Don does not lose track of friends or mentors. And, we were delighted when he attended Don's 70th birthday party and wore a yarmulke. As one of the invited speakers, he told the delightful story of how the three of us had met some 10 years earlier.

Don and Judy have been creating and writing "Hadassah: A Story That Could Be True," a drama based on the Bible book of Esther. The story has a strong multicultural and interfaith theme and storyline. Mel has been a valuable consultant in this creative energy, which may be coming to a stage or movie theater near you. Stay tuned …

Mel Gregory and Dr. Beverly Vaughn

Rabbi Jonathan Sacks once wrote:

"Jews became the people whose heroes were teachers, whose citadels were schools, and whose passion was study and the life of the mind." Mel Gregory walks that walk as a leader and elder of his Seventh Day Adventist congregation in Newtonville, NJ.

Chapter 29

Jewish Holidays: "They tried to kill us. We survived. Let's eat."

We celebrate all of the Jewish holidays with varying degrees of participation. We are fond of Hanukkah and have a big party with our extended family, gifts, and kosher food right in our Jewish home in Mays Landing.

In 2023, we celebrated Rosh Hashanah and Yom Kippur by singing in the choir on the bima and observing many of the traditions of these High Holy Days. Pesach is a favorite as we get together with friends for the second Seder. We also participate in the Purim basket exchange and are looking forward to Purim spiels in the years to come.

Chapter 30

Fun Facts to Know about Beth El Synagogue of Margate City, NJ

Our Beth El Synagogue is a Conservative shul. We are inclusive, egalitarian, and often known as "the hamisch shul," that is, "a friendly, welcoming, and inclusive congregation, having qualities associated with a homelike atmosphere; simple, warm, relaxed, cozy, unpretentious."

Buildings are not usually the most important thing about a Jewish community. However, the building that houses our shul is impressive.

Hopefully, someone will write the history of Beth El Synagogue someday. But today is not that day. Meanwhile, here are some fun facts to know.

1. Beth El Synagogue was founded in 1958 and has been operating continuously since 1961.
2. Rabbi Fishman was the first rabbi. Among other aspects of his leadership, he found ways to include women on the bima, including reading from the Torah and Bat Mitzvah services.
3. Harry Klinghoffer was the first synagogue president.
4. As the years progressed, Margate City opened and developed Beth El, the Jewish Community Center, Emeth Shalom, the Hebrew Academy, and Beth Israel.

5. Holocaust Survivors who had settled in New Jersey and who were raising families in the Atlantic County area contributed their resources, dedication, and leadership abilities to synagogue life.

6. Jewish War Veterans have also been a significant energy and force in synagogue life.

7. Rabbi Aaron Krauss first joined us in 1983 and has been a religious, civic, and spiritual leader for over 40 years.

8. We have a long history of religious education, bar mitzvah, bat mitzvah, and new members who have joined us over the years, including people who have converted to Judaism.

9. Cantor Goren and Tammy S. have guided more than six new converts in the past several years.

10. Fundraising activities have resurfaced during and after the devastating impact of the COVID-19 pandemic. We have held successful golf tournaments and fundraising activities at the Harbor Pines Golf Club, owned and operated by the Gurwicz family.

11. The Gurwicz family has been one of the most influential and important families for Don and Judy Cassidy. Mitchell and especially Ed have been especially important to the legacy and ongoing survival of our synagogue. We are happy to count them among our friends. From the first day we walked through the front door, we noticed the names of Max and Lola Gurwicz, Ed's parents, over the entrance. We are honored to share the

legacy of their family's many initiatives and contributions to our synagogue.

Max and Lola Gurwicz Building

12. The Choir: Organized Chaos on the Bima. Beth El's choir is directed and conducted by Cantor Goren. We had wanted to be part of it ever since we first heard them sing many years ago, and now it is one of the many joys of our synagogue life. During High Holy Day services in the autumn of 2023, we dressed in our new white choir robes and did our very best to add energy to this sacred music. The rhythms, melodies, harmonies, and energies astound us, and we feel honored to be a part of this special choir.

Our B'nai Mitzvah

On Saturday, November 15, 2025, Judy and I were blessed to have our B'nai Mitzvah at Beth El Synagogue. More than 30 people were there, but who's counting?

In addition to synagogue friends, we were blessed by the presence of our daughter, Meghan, and her two sons, Clark and Jack, who drove all the way from Maryland to celebrate with us. Also, Judy's cousin, Ann, drove from Pennsylvania to be with us.

We had studied for six months with Cantor Ralph Goren to become fully prepared for my Bar Mitzvah and Judy's Bat Mitzvah. Our combined ceremony was called a B'nai Mitzvah, which literally translates in English to "children of the commandment."

Our Hebrew teacher, Tammy, and other members of our Beth El choir assured us when it was all over that we had done very well. Of special note was our dear Rabbi Krauss, who not only participated fully with us, but also gave a beautiful sermon and other powerful words and presented us with a certificate of achievement, which we now have on a wall in our home.

As part of our B'nai Mitzvah, Don gave his interpretation of the Haftorah showing that Avraham was a "man of action" who led his people by example, not merely words. Judy focused on how important it was that Avraham instructed that the search for Isaac's prospective bride be to find a woman who would be respectful of others and be respectable because of her nature of thinking of the needs of others.

Chapter 31

Our Family of Origin: L'dor V'dor

All faith traditions honor family and friends. Judaism has intentional traditions that are powerful. The commandment to honor parents happens each year as we celebrate the yehrzeits, the anniversaries of the deaths of our parents. This was especially sad as we mourned the loss of Judy's mom, Gloria.

Jewish Wedding Ceremony, February 2022

Our extended family on both sides of our marriage and blended family means more to us than words can accurately express. We are incredibly blessed that our relatives have embraced our conversion. Nearly all of our family have been to Beth El for one simchah or another: Tom, Angela, Jeanette, Jim, Gloria, Gloriajean, Meghan, Kyle, Jude, Johanna, Jason, Kelly, Knight, Clark, Jack, Kelly, Brien, Conor, Teddy,

Betty, Jimmy, Ann, and many other family and friends like Jack, Barbara, Billy and Anne.

Only one week before this book was about to go to its first printing in its first edition, we received a surprise phone call from Judy's sister, Gloria Jean, and her daughter-in-law, Alyssa.

These two wonderful family members are not Jewish, and we had gifted them a 6-foot-tall, framed brass rubbing, which had been in our house for many, many years.

We had mistakenly thought that this brass rubbing was of the famous Irishman, Patrick, also known as Saint Patrick.

However, right after we gifted the brass rubbing from our house to Alyssa and Jake's house, they made a startling discovery that this was not Saint Patrick at all, and was instead someone very deeply connected to the Holocaust.

Family Hanukkah Party

Chapter 32

The Stockton Connection: Beth El and Stockton University grow up together

Many personal, institutional, and storied connections join Richard Stockton State College (now Stockton University) and the Beth El Synagogue together. You could say they are like cousins who grew up in the same neighborhood . . . in and out of each other's kitchens and back yards with a deep Atlantic City and Margate City story together from the very beginning.

Harvey Kesselman has been with Stockton since it opened. He was a student in the first year in 1971, a professor, a dean, a Vice President, the Provost, the President, and always a dear friend of Beth El Synagogue for all of those 50+ years. How fitting it was that Beth El Synagogue hosted a major tribute to his career on May 31, 2023, honoring his retirement as President of Stockton University. Harvey is a visionary leader, and many of the aspects that make Stockton a student-centered place to learn grew out of his vision and his leadership.

Equally appropriate is that the legendary Dr. Beverly Vaughn was the master of ceremonies at Harvey's celebration because her visionary leadership at Stockton and many, many contributions to the music and culture, and the deep connection between Stockton and Beth El are directly attributable to Bev. We enjoyed singing in the Stockton Oratorio Society production of "The Messiah" held in Atlantic City one year, conducted and directed by Bev. But, most of all, we have felt that our four years at Stockton were greatly enriched by her being a friend and mentor for both of us.

Beverly Vaughn and Judy Cassidy at Stockton

Yitzhak Sharon and Gayle Rosenthal have been deeply connected with Stockton and Beth El. In our 4 years at Stockton, there were several Jewish faculty and staff members who ended up with a deep connection to Beth El. In my role as Director of Counseling in the Wellness Center, I had the fortune to receive referrals from staff members to help students.

Yitzhak, in his role as Professor, and Gayle, in her roles as a teacher and also the Director of the Holocaust Resource Center, both referred numerous students to be helped by the Wellness Center. They both have lived very strongly in chessed and tikkun olam.

Chapter 33

What We Left Behind: Baruch Hashem.

People ask us if there has been anything difficult about converting from Christianity to Judaism. Activities that we miss involve the secular aspects of Christianity. We truly miss decorating a Christmas tree. And, we still dye eggs in the spring. But, there is nothing actually Christian about Santa, a Christmas tree, or the Easter Bunny.

Historically, ignorance, greed, and fear were key ingredients of antisemitism. One need only look back in history to the destructive power of the Crusades and the Spanish Inquisition to see how the original, gentle message of Christianity was twisted by angry atheists and rage-filled anti-Semites.

We were shocked to recently discover a book which is never mentioned or talked about, even in our own Lutheran experience, because it is so shockingly anti-Semitic that the reader can scarcely believe it was written by the great Roman Catholic priest, Martin Luther, in his later years in Germany over 500 years ago.

We do not include the title of that book because its name does not deserve the honor of being mentioned here. Suffice it to say that Adolf Hitler held Martin Luther's book in one hand, while he shouted at Lutheran pastors, and tried to convince them to become part of his horrific vision of the future, called The Final Solution. It is notable that although the Lutheran Church in Germany did not protest against Nazism, some individual Lutheran ministers went to their death rather than join the horrible and un-Christian activities that eventually became known as the Shoah, the Holocaust. So, we really don't regret leaving formal Christianity behind.

In addition, no thinking person can actually believe that it was the Jews who killed Jesus. Scholarly history books convince us that it was the Romans who killed Jesus and nailed him to a cross. They feared that Jesus would lead his people to overthrow the Roman government, which was never his intention. This is a documented historical fact and should have finally been addressed in 1964. The Pope at Vatican 2 was able to change the course of this aspect of history. Correction, this horrible misconception and perversion of history.

So, the next time you hear anyone say that the Jews killed Jesus, we invite you to ask them this question: "Where did you read that?" They won't be able to tell you. And, as I have done many times in the past five years, it is a great opportunity to gently correct them and simply say, "No, the Romans killed Jesus."

People of all three Abrahamic religions worship and pray to God, whether we say, "God the Father," or "Adonai," or "Allah."

God does not really care what we call him, but does want us to love one another and treat each other well, and "learn war no more."

Chapter 34

Our Jewish House and Home

Some outward signs of our Jewish home include our Menorah, which lights up brightly on our front lawn in November and December. The Hanukkah menorah is so bright that airplanes coming into the Atlantic City International Airport can use our 6-foot-tall Menorah as a navigational point!

Mezuzahs await our entry and exit on the door frames of many exterior and interior doorways. Our Jewish wedding certificate stands in a frame on the mantlepiece in our living room.

The indoor aspects of our Jewish home include Kosher food and shelves filled with books on Jewish history, philosophy, and religion, including more than 30 by Rabbi Jonathan Sacks. We have framed certificates and wall hangings. We also enjoy family gatherings at Chanukkah, religious holidays, and birthdays.

Holiday Fun

Chapter 35

Not the Final Chapter: "Collect Mentors"

This brief chapter pays tribute to people who have inspired, guided, and educated both of us in our professional careers and in our faith journeys.

Dr. John Breeskin once said to Don, "Collect mentors. Stay in touch with them throughout your life as they are valuable now and will continue to be important people in your life story."

Our mentors from Stockton University and Beth El Synagogue include Dr. Rose Scaffitti, Dr. Beverly Vaughn, Dr. Harvey Kesselman, Dr. Norm Chazin, Cantor Ralph Goren, Tammy S., Gerry S., Judy S., Mel Gregory, and Rabbi Aaron Krauss.

Dozens of others could be named, as they have helped us along in our journeys.

Our mentors have our deepest respect, love, and gratitude for their countless efforts and acts of generosity. We hope to stay in touch with all of you now and in olam haba.

Chapter 36

Hadassah: A Story That Could Be True (A Purim Spielberg)

Don woke up slowly from a stunning dream on Monday, September 25, 2023, Yom Kippur. Out of total darkness arose the sound of hundreds of people singing The Shema. The prayer faded away into a peaceful feeling as the first light of dawn emerged.

As the week progressed, a musical drama emerged, a revision of the story of Esther in The Tanach (the Hebrew Bible) and the Christian Bible. This powerful story of good triumphing over evil and of dreams that come true has survived for thousands of years. These themes also appear in stories of many cultures throughout history.

In **Hadassah: A Story That Could Be True**, using revisionist history, Esther's story grows and transforms with the addition of several important main characters and hundreds of additional minor characters.

Queen Esther is called "Hadassah" in this historical fiction and is joined by two other strong women. Vashti is banished to Ethiopia, where she meets Queen Makeda, an ancestor of the Queen of Sheba. Vashti and Makeda travel back to Shushan and bring courage and hope to Hadassah's story and to our own world, which needs to "study war no more" now more than ever.

As the weeks and months of October and November 2023 progressed, this story tried to become a Purim spiel script for our synagogue in Margate, New Jersey.

It failed.

Hadassah: A Story That Could Be True wasn't funny. Also, three surprise plot twists emerged that refused to meet the requirements of a revenge story in which the villain dies the death that he had planned for one of the story's heroes.

In nearly every Purim spiel enacted by nearly every synagogue, the catharsis of "booing" Haman and his treachery while condoning the deaths of his sons gives some audience members the illusion of justice and the satisfaction of revenge.

"Hadassah" refuses to end like that.

Furthermore, this story brings an intergenerational theme as young leaders from three different nations surprise us with an ending to the crisis in the story.

In this new story, a message emerges that the best revenge is to live peacefully and to live well.

And that's our story.

SECTION FOUR
Appendix

Appendix 1
Conversion 101: How Wandering Converts can become Wandering Jews

For those of you who have not made the choice to be chosen, but might be interested in doing so, we invite you to CONTACT US.

Not all synagogues, and not all religions or faith communities, are welcoming to strangers and outsiders. But don't let that stop you from pursuing a conversion. Formal conversion is not easy, but it is possible. Who knew?

Go to synagogue. Pray. Talk to the rabbi, the cantor, and the friendly people who stay for the meal after the service.

One of the best books about the conversion process is "Choosing Judaism" by Lydia Kukoff.

Another recommended book is "A Jewish Girl & A Not-So-Jewish Boy," written by Sandra M. Z. Armstrong.

CONTACT US: cassidyphd@gmail.com

Special Thanks

Special Thanks to Rabbi Aaron Krauss, Cantor Ralph Goren, Gerry S. Judy S., Judy Landau, James Landau, Laurene Stopper, Ron Cruz, Tammy S., Lee S., Denise Borisch, Eve Kleiner, Al Kleiner, Mitchell Gurwicz, Ed Gurwicz and many, many other people who have given us their time, their prayers and their love.

This story is dedicated to our parents, our children and their spouses, and our grandchildren all of whom are teaching us many things that are important to know. We see them and want them to know how much they are seen. We hear them and want them to know how their voices ring through the day, through the week, through the years, l'dor v'dor.

Thank you Rabbi Angela Buchdahl for your visionary leadership at Central Synagogue. Your book, "Heart of a Stranger," has added wisdom, joy, and hope to all of our lives. We are especially pleased that your view about being the chosen people is either the same or very similar to our own view in chapter 22 of our book. We selected the subtitle of our book more than two years ago when our book was in an earlier draft! Yesterday, as I was about to tell my editor to send this book to the printer, I encountered your words on this delicate topic of "choice." We hope to meet you in person when we come to Central Synagogue to visit with our friend Andrew Miller, and his family.

Resources

Websites

Rabbisacks.org

maccabeats.com

Ashreiwellness.com

Email

cassidyphd@gmail.com